PHILIP COLLINS

RADIOS

PHOTOGRAPHS BY SAM SARGENT

A BOOK OF POSTCARDS

Pomegranate

SAN FRANCISCO

D1519008

Pomegranate Communications, Inc.
Box 6099, Rohnert Park, CA 94927
800-227-1428
www.pomegranate.com

Pomegranate Europe Ltd.
Fullbridge House, Fullbridge
Maldon, Essex CM9 4LE
England

ISBN 0-7649-2039-1
Pomegranate Catalog No. AA155

Text © 2002 Philip Collins
Photographs © 2002 Sam Sargent

Pomegranate publishes books of
postcards on a wide range of subjects.
Please contact the publisher for more information.

Cover designed by Ronni Madrid
Printed in China
10 09 08 07 06 05 04 03 02   10 9 8 7 6 5 4 3 2 1

To facilitate detachment of the postcards from this book, fold each card along its perforation line before tearing.

Before 1950, radio exerted an influence on America that equaled that of the railroad and the automobile. The rail network created cities and structured our economic lives. Later the automobile moved many people to the suburbs, the postwar economy, and a new consumer status. But radio shaped the American mind and its imagination.

Jack Benny, Fibber McGee & Molly, and Amos 'n Andy put a smile on the nation's faces in dark days. The Shadow conjured mysterious superhuman influences at work. The naive messages from the Lone Ranger and Dick Tracy had a spine of truth, justice, and the American way. Little wonder that so many of us share a shameless nostalgia for a simpler time. Our youth.

When we listened at home, the radio receivers were primitive objects—by today's high-tech standards—though they did the job. As technical advances improved the interior mechanism, the whole set could be made lighter and smaller. Radio design plots an advancement from the cumbersome wooden consoles of the twenties and thirties to the matchbox-size receivers of today that can fit into a very small pocket.

The designs featured here represent a cross section of three decades of radio cabinet aesthetics. Their elegance and sometimes whimsy is uniquely American. Very few models from overseas manufacturers could rival the imaginative appeal and flair of the U.S. companies and industrial designers.

The infinite variation of cabinet design over a period of thirty years offers the collector the continual prospect of finding something new and sometimes undocumented. Vintage radio collecting has mushroomed in the United States. To find a fifty-year-old radio that approaches mint condition is rare indeed, and treasured by the collector, but much else can be treasured and even returned to good order. There are specialists now who enjoy comfortable careers as restorers and manufacturers of replication parts, such as knobs, dial glasses, trims, handles, and cosmetic adornments that time has not treated well.

In only eleven years, between 1930 and 1941, an estimated 71 million home radio receivers were sold in the United States. I have about 350 of them. They are a pleasure to hear as well as see, today and in the mind's eye of my youth, in equal measure.

—Philip Collins

RADIOS

Stewart Warner "World's Fair" Model R-108, 1933
"A Century of Progress" special design
Metal
Philip Collins Collection

BOX 6099   ROHNERT PARK   CA 94927

Pomegranate

Text © Philip Collins
Photograph © Sam Sargent

RADIOS

Radio Glo, c. 1935
Glass and chromed metal on a wood base
Courtesy Harvey's, Melrose Avenue, Los Angeles

BOX 6099   ROHNERT PARK   CA 94927

Pomegranate

Text © Philip Collins
Photograph © Sam Sargent

RADIOS

Stewart Warner "Good Companion" Model R-192, 1936
Metal cabinet; chrome pillars
Klaus Beckmann Collection

BOX 6099   ROHNERT PARK   CA 94927

Pomegranate

Text © Philip Collins
Photograph © Sam Sargent

RADIOS

Kadette "Classic," 1936
Top left: **Model K14**
Top right: **Model K16**
Bottom left: **Model K13**
Bottom right: **Model K10**
Victor Keen Collection

CA 94927

ROHNERT PARK

BOX 6099

Pomegranate

Text © Philip Collins
Photograph © Sam Sargent

RADIOS

Fada Model 246G, 1937
Philip Collins Collection

BOX 6099   ROHNERT PARK   CA 94927

Pomegranate

Text © Philip Collins
Photograph © Sam Sargent

RADIOS

Pilot "Lone Ranger" Model G-160, c. 1937
Wood
Kris Gimmy Collection

CA 94927

ROHNERT PARK

BOX 6099

Pomegranate

Text © Philip Collins
Photograph © Sam Sargent

RADIOS

Silvertone Model 6178A, c. 1938
Philip Collins Collection

CA. 94927

ROHNERT PARK

BOX 6099

Pomegranate

Text © Philip Collins
Photograph © Sam Sargent

RADIOS

Silvertone Model 6110, 1938
Designed by Clarence Karstadt
Refinished
Philip Collins Collection

BOX 6099 ROHNERT PARK CA 94927

Pomegranate

Text © Philip Collins
Photograph © Sam Sargent

RADIOS

RCA, c. 1938
Export model from Chile
Philip Collins Collection

BOX 6099 · ROHNERT PARK · CA 94927

Pomegranate

Text © Philip Collins
Photograph © Sam Sargent

RADIOS

Philco "Transitone" Model UA 52P, c. 1938
Restored; new tuning dial
Philip Collins Collection

CA 94927

ROHNERT PARK

BOX 6099

Pomegranate

Text © Philip Collins
Photograph © Sam Sargent

RADIOS

RCA "San Francisco Expo" Model 40 x 57, 1939
Pressed wood facing; wood cabinet
Bruce and Charlotte Mager Collection

BOX 6099 ROHNERT PARK CA 94927

Pomegranate

Text © Philip Collins
Photograph © Sam Sargent

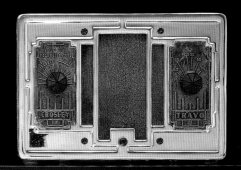

RADIOS

Top left: **Perwal Model #52,** 1937
Top right: **Crosley "Travo" 166,** 1933
Bottom left: **Arvin Model 522A,** 1941
Bottom right: **Sparton,** c. 1940
Metal chromed
Philip Collins Collection

BOX 6099   ROHNERT PARK   CA 94927

Pomegranate

Text © Philip Collins
Photograph © Sam Sargent

RADIOS

RCA "La Siesta" Model 40 x 53, 1939
Wood
Barry and Ellen Blum Collection

BOX 6099   ROHNERT PARK   CA 94927

Pomegranate

Text © Philip Collins
Photograph © Sam Sargent

RADIOS

Kadette "Topper" Model L-25, 1940
Bambi and David Mednick Collection

BOX 6099   ROHNERT PARK   CA 94927

Pomegranate

Text © Philip Collins
Photograph © Sam Sargent

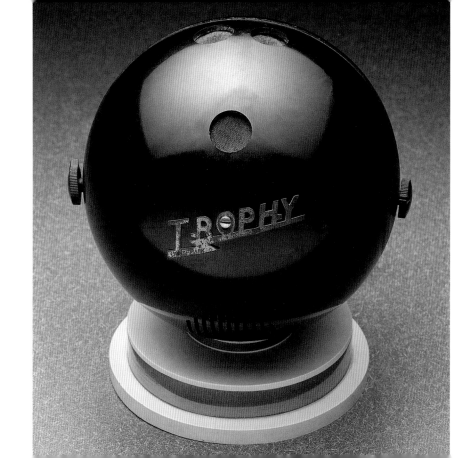

RADIOS

Trophy "Bowling Ball," c. 1941
Bruce and Charlotte Mager Collection

BOX 6099   ROHNERT PARK   CA 94927

Pomegranate

Text © Philip Collins
Photograph © Sam Sargent

RADIOS

Majestic Model 52, c. 1946
Philip Collins Collection

BOX 6099   ROHNERT PARK   CA 94927

Pomegranate

Text © Philip Collins
Photograph © Sam Sargent

RADIOS

Airline Model 62-455, 1946
Philip Collins Collection

BOX 6099   ROHNERT PARK   CA 94927

Pomegranate

Text © Philip Collins
Photograph © Sam Sargent

RADIOS

Remler Model 5506 (left) **and Model 5500** (right), 1947
Philip Collins Collection

BOX 6099   ROHNERT PARK   CA 94927

Pomegranate

Text © Philip Collins
Photograph © Sam Sargent

RADIOS

Airline Model 84BR 1508B, 1946
Kay Tornborg Collection

BOX 6099 ROHNERT PARK CA 94927

Pomegranate

Text © Philip Collins
Photograph © Sam Sargent

RADIOS

Remler Model 5300, 1947
Philip Collins Collection

BOX 6099   ROHNERT PARK   CA 94927

Pomegranate

Text © Philip Collins
Photograph © Sam Sargent

RADIOS

Emerson Model 540, 1947
Philip Collins Collection

BOX 6099   ROHNERT PARK   CA 94927

Pomegranate

Text © Philip Collins
Photograph © Sam Sargent

RADIOS

Delco Model R-1238, 1948
Philip Collins Collection

BOX 6099   ROHNERT PARK   CA 94927

Pomegranate

Text © Philip Collins
Photograph © Sam Sargent

RADIOS

DeWald Model B512, 1948
Philip Collins Collection

BOX 6099   ROHNERT PARK   CA 94927

Pomegranate

Text © Philip Collins
Photograph © Sam Sargent

RADIOS

Northern Electric Model 5002 Series, c. 1948
Philip Collins Collection

Pomegranate

BOX 6099   ROHNERT PARK   CA 94927

Text © Philip Collins
Photograph © Sam Sargent

RADIOS

Philco "Transitone" Model 48-230, 1948
Philip Collins Collection

BOX 6099 ROHNERT PARK CA 94927

Pomegranate

Text © Philip Collins
Photograph © Sam Sargent

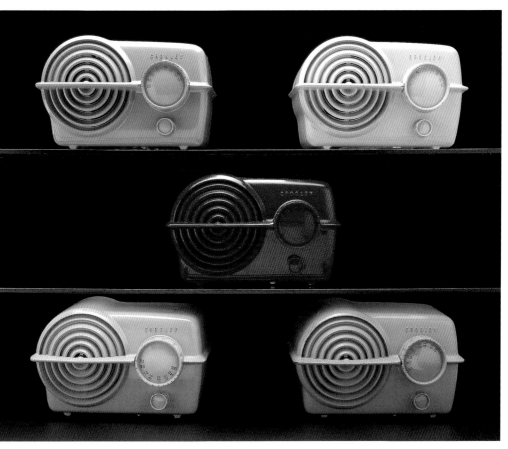

RADIOS

Crosley Models 11-114 through 11-118U, 1951
Barry and Ellen Blum Collection (top left and right, bottom right)
Philip Collins Collection (center and bottom left)

BOX 6099   ROHNERT PARK   CA 94927

Pomegranate

Text © Philip Collins
Photograph © Sam Sargent

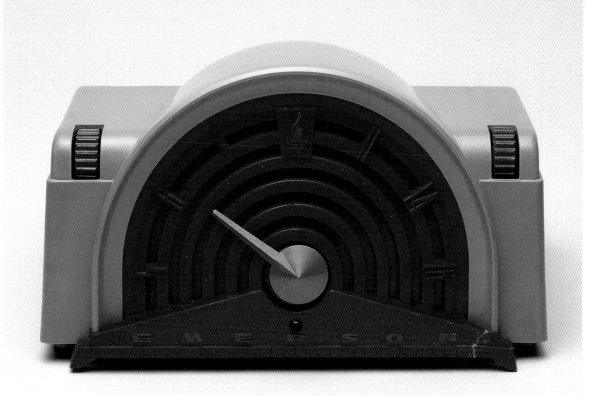

RADIOS

Emerson Model 744-B, 1954
Philip Collins Collection

BOX 6099 ROHNERT PARK CA 94927

Pomegranate

Text © Philip Collins
Photograph © Sam Sargent

RADIOS

Zenith Model T402 (left), **Model T400** (center), and **Model M403**
(right), c. 1955
Barry and Ellen Blum Collection

BOX 6099 ROHNERT PARK CA 94927

Pomegranate

Text © Philip Collins
Photograph © Sam Sargent

RADIOS

Motorola Model 57 CC, 1957 (top), and **Model 56 CD,** 1956 (bottom)
Philip Collins Collection

BOX 6099 ROHNERT PARK CA 94927

Pomegranate

Text © Philip Collins
Photograph © Sam Sargent

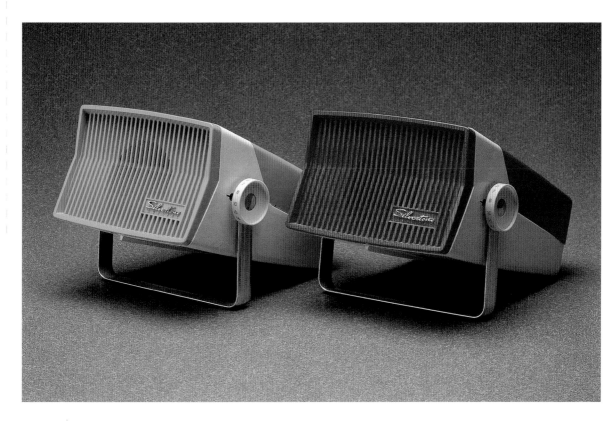

RADIOS

Silvertone Model 8218 (left) and **Model 8219** (right), c. 1959
Barry and Ellen Blum Collection

BOX 6099   ROHNERT PARK   CA 94927

Pomegranate

Text © Philip Collins
Photograph © Sam Sargent